Let's tell the TIME

Written by Daryl Stuart
Illustrated by David Moss

GALLERY BOOKS
An Imprint of W. H. Smith Publishers Inc.
112 Madison Avenue
New York City 10016

Seven o'clock. The alarm rings.
What shall I do today?

Seven thirty. Time for breakfast.
Please may I have some juice,
Mom?

Eight o'clock and time to meet my friends at playschool.

Ten o'clock. We're hard at work...
having fun!

Eleven o'clock. Time for a morning walk.

Twelve o'clock. Lunchtime! Mmmm! That walk made me so hungry.

One o'clock. Mom is waiting at the gate to take me home.

Two o'clock. I go to the library and shopping with Mom.

Three o'clock and I help Mom carry the shopping.

Four o'clock. That's the time the TV programs are specially for me!

Five o'clock. Dinner time. I enjoy helping Mom.

Splish splash! **Six o'clock** is bathtime for the ducks and me!

6:00

Seven o'clock and Dad reads me a story.
Sometimes I fall asleep.

Eight o'clock and I'm asleep.

While I'm asleep I don't see the clock, but I know that it goes on ticking all night long.